The New Novello Choral Edition
NOVELLO HANDEL EDITION

General Editor   Donald Burrows

In the Lord put I my trust
(HWV 247)

'Chandos' Anthem No.2

Tenor Soloist, SATB* Chorus and Orchestra

*Handel's original STB Choruses are available separately in this edition as NOV060137-03

Edited by Damian Cranmer

Vocal Score

Order No. NOV060137

NOVELLO PUBLISHING LIMITED
14 - 15 Berners Street, London, W1T 3LJ

It is requested that on all concert notices and programmes
acknowledgement is made to 'The Novello Handel Edition'.

*Es wird gebeten, auf sämtlichen Konzertankündigungen und
Programmen 'The Novello Handel Edition' als Quelle zu erwähnen.*

Il est exigé que toutes notices et programmes de concerts,
comportent des remerciements à 'The Novello Handel Edition'.

Permission to reproduce the Preface of this Edition must be obtained from the Publisher.

*Die Erlaubnis, das Vorwort dieser Ausgabe oder Teile desselben zu
reproduzieren, muß beim Verlag eingeholt werden.*

Le droit de reproduction de ce document à partir de la préface doit être obtenu de l'éditeur.

Orchestral material is available on hire from the Publisher.
The full score and parts are also available for sale as
NOV060137-01 and NOV060137-02 respectively.

*Orchestermaterial ist beim Verlag erhältlich.
Die Partitur und die Stimmen dieser Ausgabe können mit folgenden Bestellnummern käuflich erworben
werde: NOV060137-01 (Partitur) und NOV060137-02 (Stimmen).*

Les partitions d'orchestre sont en location disponibles chez l'éditeur.
La partition et matériels pour cette publication sont aussi disponibles à l'achat : numero de
catalogue NOV060137-01 (partition) et NOV060137-02 (matériels)

CONTENTS

Preface			v
1	Sinfonia		1
2	Chorus	In the Lord put I my trust	5
3	Tenor Solo	God is a constant sure defence	16
4	Chorus	Behold the wicked bend their bow	19
5	Tenor Solo	But God, who hears the suff'ring poor	27
6	Chorus	Snares, fire and brimstone on their heads	30
7	Tenor Solo	The righteous Lord	35
8	Chorus	Then shall my song, with praise inspir'd	38

Approximate duration
20 minutes

INSTRUMENTATION

Oboe
Bassoon
Strings (Violin 1, Violin 2, [Cello], Double Bass)
Continuo (Organ or Harpsichord)

The performing material for this edition
includes a fully-realised Continuo part.

PREFACE

THE CANNONS ANTHEMS

The eleven anthems which Handel wrote for James Brydges, Earl of Carnarvon, date from 1717 and 1718. Commonly known as the "Chandos" Anthems, they have in recent times been referred to as Cannons Anthems because they were all written before Brydges was created Duke of Chandos in 1719. They were also written before the completion of the chapel for the grand house which Brydges was building at Cannons near Edgware, and so the anthems were given in the neighbouring church of St Lawrence Whitchurch, Little Stanmore. The scale of Brydges' plans for his residence was enormous, but the results of his labours were short-lived. The music at Cannons gradually reduced in the 1720s after the sudden decline of the Duke's investments in the disaster of the South Sea Bubble. The estate never fully recovered and the house had been demolished by 1750, following the sale by the Duke's son of most of its valuable contents. If the musical resources available to Handel were small, in most cases one to a part (though the top line may have been sung by up to three boys), it should be remembered that a music establishment even on this scale was unique in private houses in England.

Handel began this series of anthems in the late summer of 1717 with a reworking of *As pants the hart* (HWV 251), which he had composed for the Chapel Royal some years earlier[1]. He wrote the anthems in pairs, one penitential and one laudatory[2], and by the end of September, four were complete and two more were on the way[3]. *In the Lord put I my trust* is the penitential anthem in the fourth pairing and was probably finished before the end of the year[4].

EDITORIAL METHOD

In the Lord put I my trust has a three-part chorus with no alto part and a high, demanding tenor line, characteristics that would exclude the work from the repertoire of many choral ensembles. This edition, however, presents the work with SATB chorus, in a version made by the editor. There has been no attempt to make a new piece; in particular, the instrumental parts have been retained without change. This means that it is possible to use the orchestral material to perform the original three-part scoring, and STB choral parts and a full score with three-part chorus are available from the publisher.

In the SATB version the original tenor line has been divided mainly between the alto and tenor, and the chorus texture expanded by using music from the instrumental parts where possible, and some free addition where not. The bass vocal line is unaltered where it follows the instrumental bass, except for one bar (No.6, b13) where the vocal bass, despite being in unison with the instrumental bass, has been given to the tenor because of the imitative possibility. If Handel had done this, he would almost certainly have rested the double bass (at least) and conductors and directors may feel that this is a good option: these four notes are indicated in the double bass part. There are three passages (No.2, bb86-90; No.4, bb46-53; No.4, bb86-91) where the bass voice becomes a second tenor line and a new vocal bass has been constructed aligned with the instrumental bass. The soprano line is mostly unchanged. There are two passages (No.6, bb19-21; No.8, bb24-25) where the top line has been given to the alto, and one passage (No.8, bb35-37) where it has been possible to extend the vocal texture upwards by the use of appropriate material from the instrumental parts.

This edition is based largely on the autograph score, but variants in the material dating from the years immediately after composition have been considered. There are two significant variants in the 1717-20 material of HWV 247. The first relates to Handel's addition of an extra bar between bars 44 and 45 of the Sinfonia[5]. In general the earlier copies follow the original and the later ones the altered version, suggesting that Handel did not make the change immediately, and possibly, though by no means certainly, when he was preparing the material for the Op.3 concertos. At any rate the change may not relate to early performances of the anthem. The original version has been used in the current edition: the revised version is:

v

The second variant concerns the cadence in bars 38 and 39 of No.3. Handel's autograph has the following:

The alternative version, adopted in the current edition, is found only in sources **C** and **D** and is given here because the vocal score does not show the full texture. Handel at least considered something like this because he wrote g′ for the tenor (note 4 in bar 38) before crossing it out and changing it to d′:

The major advantage of the alternative version is the violin 2 c♯″ in bar 38, which provides the anacrusis to the melodic pattern found in all other statements[6]. The second version cannot be a scribe's error. In all there are some thirteen instances where the early sources (**C**, **D**, **E** and **F**) give a different reading from the autograph and show some measure of agreement with each other, although they also have enough discrepancies to eliminate the possibility that they are a chain of copies. Taken together with variants in other anthems in these sources, for example the inclusion in source **D** of 'The

Celebrated Trio' in *My Song shall be alway* HWV 252, this begins to suggest, as Graydon Beeks has pointed out, that some now lost material, possibly for performance at Cannons, was the basis for these early copies. The violist and copyist D. Linike produced scores of the anthems (Lbl Add. MS. 29417-29426, source **G**) in 1725/6, and there is evidence that he used Handel's autograph as his source, even that he made additions to Handel's score, particularly to the verbal underlay in the chorus parts[7]. It would be good to say that all later scores follow the autograph or this Linike copy, but it's not quite as simple as that. The Cannons Anthems will, no doubt, repay much further study, but the extent to which Handel oversaw the preparation of particular copies of his works may remain elusive.

Handel used soprano clef (C1) and tenor clef (C4) for the upper voices and these have been modernised. Key signatures are as Handel wrote them. Editorial additions, such as movement headings, dynamics and trills, are in square brackets; added ties and slurs have a cross stroke. Suggested rhythmic changes are indicated by 'flag' stems above, and occasionally below, the stave. Hemiolas in triple time movements are indicated by square brackets above and below the system.

The aim of the keyboard reduction is to give a representation of the orchestral texture without posing too many demands on the player. Right-hand semiquaver scales in sixths, for example, have been omitted. Where the organ continuo would be expected to fill out the texture, small notes have been used to complete the harmony. At all times the lowest note in the left hand is the continuo bass at the pitch at which Handel wrote it.

BORROWINGS

The Sinfonia of *In the Lord put I my trust* is best known as the first two movements of the Concerto Grosso in D minor Op.3 No.5[8]. That the oboe part of the *allegro* is written on a separate page from the string score, and that the whole of the movement is written on different paper from the rest of the anthem[9], gives at least the possibility that the Sinfonia was not written at the same time as the anthem. There is also the matter of the extra bar which Handel added to his score. This extra bar is found where the same music is used in the opening of the third movement of the sixth Keyboard Suite in F-sharp minor which was published in late 1720, but the bar is not found in the early extant copies of the anthem (sources **B**, **C**, **D**, **E** and **F**). Handel frequently reused the first bars of a movement and then allowed his improvising nature to take over, and this is the case in the Keyboard Suite, where only the first ten bars follow the Sinfonia very closely. This is also the case in the tenor solo 'God is a constant sure defence'. The duet nature of the first four bars of 'To thee Cherubin and Seraphim' from the Utrecht Te Deum is turned into a solo movement with the instrumental parts having an integral part of the imitative texture. This music is foreshadowed in the earlier duet *Se tu non lasci amore* HWV 193, and turns up in another guise in 'O death, where is thy sting' from *Messiah*. The choral movements Nos. 4 and 6 derive from music in the *Brockes Passion* HWV 48, 'Greift zu, schlagt todt' and the *allegro* of 'O weh, sie binden ihn' respectively. In both cases, Handel expanded the music for *In the Lord put I my trust*, but when he used the music again in *Deborah*, he went back to the Passion version. The appearance of the opening phrase of 'God's tender mercy' in 'When thou art nigh' from *Susanna* (now in the major) scarcely merits a mention under this heading.

CONTINUO AND BASS INSTRUMENTS
In the choral movements (Nos 2, 4, 6 and 8) Handel wrote a separate line for bassoon and double bass. The lowest (continuo) line he marked 'Organo'. The Sinfonia and the three Tenor solos have one line for the bass instruments. In the Sinfonia he marked the bass line 'Bassi'; in the three Tenor solo movements there is no marking. In the chorus movements, the bassoon, double bass and continuo mostly have the same music, and yet Handel has written out the parts fully. One can wonder why; and certainly some of his scribes did, because several of the later copies conflate the three parts on to one or two lines or leave the bassoon and double bass staves blank with directions such as 'col org', and consequently miss some of the subtlety in Handel's writing. There is little trouble in following Handel's intentions in the choral movements, and his practice in the use of clefs may give some further clues. In these movements, there are six instances where Handel uses the tenor clef (C4) for the continuo line because the Bass voice is silent and the continuo follows the Tenor voice. In all these cases, the double bass is silent and the line is covered by violin 2 (4 times)

or bassoon (twice). That the change of clef is not random can be seen from the fact that the bassoon part continues in the bass clef in both instances. This does suggest that, in the other movements, the use of the tenor clef implies rests for the double bass, which concords with many instances in Handel's work. The survival of a double bass part of the Anthems (source **F**) is interesting, but does not clarify things greatly[10]. In the Sinfonia, this part continues through the tenor clef passages. In No.3, the part has rests from the second beat of bar 13 ('solo' in the organ line) to the first three quavers of bar 21 (sensible, though not indicated by Handel), but includes the two passages of tenor clef writing (not so sensible, and shown with editorial rests in the current edition). Nos 5 and 7 have no C4 passages or solo markings in the continuo: in line with NHE practice, editorial indications of passages for reduced continuo support have been marked. No.7 includes the only passages in the Cannons Anthems where the continuo line follows the Tenor solo (bars 44-48 and 58-62). Given that Handel scrupulously rests the double bass in such passages in the choral movements, there is a particularly good case for doing so in this movement. The editor's suggestions are included in the full score and the double bass part. A further example of Handel's care with clefs in the continuo line can be found in the Sinfonia bar 84, where he has crossed out the last note (a, middle line C4), inserted a bass clef and replaced the same note, almost certainly indicating the point at which the double bass rejoins.

More importantly, the four instances where the C4 organ part is the same as violin 2 give rise to some doubts as to whether Handel intended a cello in the anthem. There is no mention of a cello in the autograph and the only other Cannons anthem not to indicate a cello is *I will magnify thee, O God my King* HWV 250a, which is the pair to *In the Lord put I my trust*. Nevertheless, a cello part has been provided for this edition and would probably be beneficial in any performance of the four-part choral version. Performances of the original three-part anthem with very small groups might do without the cello.

As with the double bass, the bassoon is clearly indicated in the choral movements. It can be assumed to play throughout the Sinfonia, as does the oboe, and for most, if not all, of No.3. If *unis[oni]* can be taken to mean violins alone on the top line of No.5, then the bassoon should be silent with the oboe. In No.7, conductors should decide whether the bassoon plays through the continuo passages or rests with the double bass. Only bars 37-43 seem an obvious case where the line should be left to cello and organ alone.

The appropriate keyboard instrument throughout the Cannons Anthems is the organ. In the vocal score, passages where there is reduced instrumentation in the bass part are shown by 'Cont.' and the return to full by 'Tutti'. All instances where there is evidence in the sources of such changes, for instance by change of clef or 'solo' marking, are shown without square brackets. Where the suggestion is entirely editorial, square brackets are used.

TEXTS

Handel chose texts for *In the Lord put I my trust* from Psalms 9, 11, 12 and 13. The first choral movement uses the Prayer Book version of Psalm 11 verse 1. The remaining movements use metrical verse taken from Tate and Brady's *New Version of the Psalms of David* (1696). In Psalm 11, Tate and Brady's versification does not quite match the Prayer Book. For the most part Handel turned to Prayer Book texts for the Cannons Anthems, but he used metrical psalms in one other, *O praise the Lord with one consent*. Fortunately he seems to have inherited from Purcell the ability to endow mediocre English verse with remarkable music. Some errors have crept in over the years: Chrysander gave 'pow'r' for 'poor' in No.5, and several copies have the plural 'servants' for 'servant' in No.8; and one unfortunate scribe wrote "lurking in a bush" for "lurking in ambush" in No.4!

The two-part structure of the psalm verse, whether in prose or metre, suited Handel's compositional style well, giving the opportunity, in the choruses, for contrasting melodic ideas which may alternate (as in Nos. 4 and 6) or combine in imitative counterpoint (as in Nos. 2 and 8). In the simpler solo movements, the break is used to form a natural half-way cadence.

SOURCES[11]

i) Autograph scores

A London, British Library, RM 2.0.d.8: ff29-59. This is Handel's autograph score. It is mostly very clearly written and has been taken as the starting point for this edition. There are few matters which have required clarification from other sources. There are two notes which

seem errors on Handel's part, both connected with alterations which he apparently did not complete, and a few accidentals which he missed. All are shown in the score or noted in the Textual Notes. As suggested above, it does seem possible that the surviving manuscripts of the period 1718-1720 were copied from now lost material, perhaps performance material, and in two cases readings from these scores have been preferred.

B London, British Library, RM 20.g.14. This is a collection of manuscripts compiled over a period of some 40 years which includes an autograph fragment of seven bars for the beginning of the *allegro* of the Sinfonia to HWV 247. It gives the version before Handel added the extra bar.

ii) Early manuscript copies to 1720

A feature of these early copies is that they show the anthems in order of composition[12]. There is no consistent ordering of the anthems after 1720 until Chrysander produced his order for source **S**, which is followed by the HWV numbering.

C London, British Library, Add.MS.62101. This is the third of three volumes which include the first eight of the Anthems, suggesting that the score may be as early as 1717. It contains HWV 247 and HWV 250a together with two anthems by Pepusch, *O sing unto the Lord* and *O be joyful*.

D The Hague, Gemeentemuseum, MS.A III 1. This is the "Cummings" score, so-called because from a few years after 1917, when it was sold as part of W. H. Cummings' collection, until 1991 it was assumed lost despite being fully described in the Museum's catalogue. It was "rediscovered" by Dorothea Schröder[13]. Inside the cover is inscribed "Contemporary transcriptions of the Chandos Anthems and Chandos Te Deum for 5 voices in B-flat. Also the Utrecht Jubilate. It was in the library of the Duke of Chandos." It does not include HWV 254 or HWV 255, the last of the anthems to be composed.

E Oxford, Bodleian Library, Tenbury MS 883 ff1-49. This is the earliest of three scores from the Tenbury collection. It is in the hand of Smith sr and dates from 1719-20. A note records the volume as belonging to Thomas Chilcott, organist of Bath in 1757. All three scores show evidence of study, at least, and possible use. For example, MS 883 has pencil pause marks in bar 83 of the Sinfonia (Vln 1 beat 2; Vln 2 beat 1) – not an example to be followed - but also corrections to the few examples of Handel's faulty part-writing.

F London, Foundling Museum, Coke Collection, ms 1254. Parts for violin 1 and contrabasso. These parts are probably connected with **D**. The two anthems not in **D** are Nos. 11 and 12 in these parts. They are useful up to a point (see above under Bass Instruments).

iii) Later manuscript copies

G London, British Library, Add.MS.29425. This is one of a set of individually bound scores (Add.MS.29417-29426) which Linike prepared shortly before his death in 1725 or 1726. Some additions which he made to the autograph score (**A**) suggest that this set of scores may have been an attempt to collate earlier material.

H Oxford, Bodleian Library, Tenbury MS 617. A landscape score in the hand of S3, c1730-35.

I London, Foundling Museum, MS 1247, Coke Collection. A score from c1740 in the hand of John Mathews, formerly part of the Earl of Shaftesbury's Collection.

J London, British Library, Egerton MS 2913, ff80-103. A volume in the hand of S3 from 1740-44 containing, in addition, HWV 255 and 'The ways of Zion do mourn'.

K London, British Library, RM 19.g.1b. This score has been given a revised catalogue number to show its relevance to RM19.g.1 (see **P**). It is by Smith from the 1740s, and together with RM19.g.1 vol.3 makes a complete set of the Cannons Anthems. It was in the library of Robert Smith, who inserted a note dated July 8th 1803 in the score, indicating that George III had given it to Dr Aylward when he was Organist at St George's, Windsor. The King was sorry that the other volume was lost. As Theodore Aylward did not take up his post at Windsor until 1788, the "lost" score (see **P** below) was already bound up matching its new fellows!

L Cambridge, Fitzwilliam Library, MS 810, pp147-197. A score from the 1740s in the hand of Smith sr.

M Hamburg, Staats- und Universitätsbibliothek, MA/177 2. This score was owned by Friedrich Chrysander and used as the basis for **S**.

N Oxford, Bodleian Library, Tenbury MSS 797, 801 and 803. The Medius Cantoris, Tenor Cantoris and Bass Cantoris of a set of part-books in which HWV 247 is Item 22.

O London, Foundling Museum, MS 1263, Coke Collection. A collection of scores, individually bound. HWV 247 is signed "script J.F. 1767". J.F is identified as Johann Fish. There is an additional note: 'This Anthem I have corrected by Mr. Handel's own score. J. Langshaw' (John Langshaw the elder 1719-1798, former owner[14]). One of the many corrections which Langshaw made was to add the extra bar in the Sinfonia.

P London, British Library, RM 19.g.1 vol 2. In the hand of S11 from c1770. RM 19.g.1 is a set of three luxuriously bound volumes, each with the same elaborate frontispiece, dated 1773. Volumes 1 and 2, in the hand of S11, may well have been prepared for this set. Volume 3 is earlier, in the hand of Smith sr, and dates from the 1740s (see **K**). The three volumes cover all of the Cannons Anthems and several Chapel Royal works.

(iv) Printed editions

Q *The Complete Score of Ten Anthems Composed Chiefly for the Chapel of his Grace the late James Duke of Chandos by G.F. Handel in three Volumes* (London: Wright & Wilkinson, 1784)

R Samuel Arnold (ed) *Anthem, in Score, Composed at Cannons, for his Grace the Duke of Chandos Between the Years 1718 & 1720. By G.F. Handel* (London c1790). Anthem X. There is some confusion in Arnold between volumes and numbers, and the numbers do not coincide with complete pieces. HWV 247 is in nos. 81 and 82. The copy with catalogue number I.50 in the British Library has been rebound with numbers on the spine. There are discrepancies between different copies of Arnold.

S F.W. Chrysander and M.Seiffert (eds), *Georg Friedrich Händels Werke: Ausgabe der Deutschen Händelgesellschaft*, (Hamburg, 1872) xxxiv pp37-78.

T Gerald Hendrie (ed), Hallische Händel-Ausgabe: *Anthems für Cannons I* (Kassel, Basel, London, 1985) pp51-100. Volume III contains a very thorough review of the sources and commentary on the variant readings for all the Cannons Anthems.

TEXTUAL NOTES

In the Notes, the pitch middle C is represented by c′, and the two octaves either side by C to B, c to b, c′ to b′ and c″ to b″.

1.Sinfonia
Bar

1   The instrumental opening is headed Sinfonia in **E**, **F**, and **I**. The marking *Largo, ma non troppo* comes from **G**; Handel wrote and crossed out *adagio* in **A**.

39   *Segue la fuga* **A**

40   *Fuga* **C**, **D**, **F**; *Allegro* **G** and most later copies. In **A** the score of the *allegro* contains only the three string parts. The oboe part is written on the following folio as a single line. The whole of the Sinfonia is written on different paper from the rest of the anthem, so perhaps this movement predates the anthem.

44   At some point, Handel made slight changes to this bar and added another bar between this and 45. He did this by making inclusion marks in the string score and also the single line oboe part, and writing the full score of the two bars on free staves at the end of the first section of the Sinfonia. The extended version is first found in a copy of the anthem in Linike's 1725/6 score (**G**), but the music in its revised form was already in existence by the end of 1720, when it appeared in the Keyboard Suite in F sharp minor. The original one-bar version, which is followed here, is found in **B C D E** and **F**, but then also in **I** and **O** (later altered). (See also above under Editorial Method.)

86   Vln 2 n2; It appears that Handel has written a flat here but added a stroke to make it into a natural. All sources except **I** and **S** give natural.

2. 'In the Lord put I my trust'
Bar

1   *Allegro moderato* from **Q**, **R**, and **S**.

11   Cont. n1; d all sources. It seems likely that Handel omitted to change the d to f when he altered notes 2 and 3 in bar 10 from Bb c.

92   **S**; **A** has no text but an extension line, words from **E**, **G**, and **H** of early sources.

103   **S**; "bird" to n1 in **A** and several later sources; to n2 in **C**, **D**, **E**, **H**, **I**, **Q**, **R** and **S**.

120-1   **A** (originally T); "as a bird" **C**, **D**. In **A**, the words "she shall flee" have been added later, perhaps by Linike. There is a possibility that the notes of these two bars are not written by Handel. In any case, all sources from **A** to **T** give nn4-5 in bar 121 as f″ g″, clashing with g″ f″ in violin 2, which follows the prevailing melodic pattern.

143   **S** n1; source **N** has e′ to avoid octaves with bass, **E** has g′.

3. 'God is a constant sure defence'
Bar

9   Cont.n8; F in **C**, **I**, **O** and **S**.

38-9   alternative cadence found in **C** and **D**. See above under Editorial Method.

4. 'Behold the wicked bend their bow'
Bar

1   *Allegro moderato* from **Q** and **R**.

24ff   "lurking in a bush", mostly corrected in a later hand to "ambush" in **H**.

30   Ob.Vln 2, S; Handel wrote this rhythm throughout as 6 quavers with ties to nn2&3 and nn4&5. Sources **J**, **N**, **P**, **Q** and **R** show some bars with slurs to nn3&4 and nn5&6.

39   T crotchet, minim in **T**.

64   T, B; dotted minim in several sources (**C**, **D**, **F** of early sources) as a reading of a rather light crotchet rest in **A** as a displaced dot.

83   S nn2-5; octave lower in **H** and **O**.

5. 'But God who hears the suff'ring poor'
Bar

14   Cont. n2; B flat in **Q**, **R** and **S**, presumably "correcting" Handel's harmony.

15   Vln n3; several sources have missed the flat.

18   After this bar, Handel originally wrote 3 bars of instrumental episode finishing in D minor, but crossed them out before continuing.

6. 'Snares, fire and brimstone on their heads'
Bar

    "Rains" for "Snares" in **H**.

18   S n5; seems to have a dot after the note in **A**, but n6 is a quaver. Only **G** and **T** have dotted rhythm.

33   T n5; c$\sharp'$ in **A** followed by several sources. Handel has changed nn3-4 from e' d' (parallel with S), and apparently omitted to change the next note.

7. 'The righteous Lord'
Bar

50   Vln 1 n2;: a' in **C, D, F, H, I, O** (originally) and **S**.

56   Cont. n2; d in **C, D, F, H, I, O** and **S**.

58   T n1; very high above the C4 clef in **A** and looks like a' without a leger line. All sources except **E** give f' which makes less successful counterpoint with the violin and oboe line.

8. 'Then shall my song, with praise inspir'd'
Bar

24   A n1; d'' in original Canto (Soprano) part.

27   S n2; **A** followed by most sources has d'', which creates parallel fifths with the bass and does not follow the melodic pattern. **E** has g'' added later, **H** has g'', and **T** adds an editorial g''.

ACKNOWLEDGEMENTS

I am grateful to the custodians and staff of the various libraries mentioned above, which house the material on which this edition is based, for permission to view their scores. Donald Burrows was most encouraging and supportive in this project which might have been thought wacky by NHE standards, and Graydon Beeks was very helpful in responding to my queries and advancing my ideas. I am grateful, too, to Novello staff, Howard Friend and Hywel Davies, who went through my score with a fine-tooth comb and made several helpful suggestions.

Damian Cranmer

1   The different versions of this anthem (and others) which Handel reworked are comprehensively surveyed in Donald Burrows, *Handel and the English Chapel Royal*, Oxford Studies in British Church Music (Oxford, 2005).

2   Graydon Beeks, 'Handel's Sacred Music' in Donald Burrows (ed) *The Cambridge Companion to Handel* (Cambridge, 1997) p172.

3   Letter from Brydges to Dr Arbuthnot. See Graydon Beeks, 'Handel and Music for the Earl of Carnarvon' in Peter Williams (ed), *Bach, Handel, Scarlatti: Tercentenary Essays* (Cambridge, 1985) p3.

4   It is indicative of the status held by the "Chandos Anthems" over nearly 300 years that the numbering of the works in the Handel catalogue is based on their Chandos connection over that of the Chapel Royal versions, some of which were earlier and all of which were grander and of larger scale. Only *O be joyful in the Lord* HWV 246 has a separate number as the Utrecht Jubilate HWV 279.

5   See Textual Notes.

6   Tenor bars 28, 33, 40; Ob. bars 32, 39; Cont bars. 40, 50.

7   See Graydon Beeks, Preface to *O praise the Lord with one consent* HWV 254 (London, 2008) and Textual Note to No.2 bars 120-1 in this edition.

8   Published by Walsh in 1734, though almost all the music is of much earlier date.

9   See Donald Burrows and Martha J. Ronish, *A Catalogue of Handel's Musical Autographs* (Oxford, 1994).

10   In the Preface to his edition of HWV 254, Graydon Beeks writes of this part: "the scribe was clearly inexperienced and there is no way of knowing whether his extraction of a double bass part from the Bassi line reflects knowledge of Handel's performance practice".

11   Much of the information on dating and scribes is taken from Gerald Hendrie (Introduction and Critical Report to **T**), Donald Burrows and Graydon Beeks.

12   For a concise discussion of the development of Donald Burrows' and his own research concerning the order of composition, see Graydon Beeks, 'Handel and Music for the Earl of Carnarvon' in Peter Williams (ed), *Bach, Handel, Scarlatti: Tercentenary Essays* (Cambridge, 1985) pp4-5.

13   See Dorothea Schröder, 'Wiederentdeckt: die Kopie der Chandos-Anthems aus der ehemahligen Sammlung Cummings' in *Göttinger Händel-Beiträge IV* (1991) pp94-107.

14   Foundling Museum Catalogue

IN THE LORD PUT I MY TRUST

GEORGE FRIDERIC HANDEL
HWV 247

No.1

SINFONIA

senza D.B.

Tutti

senza D.B.　　　　　Tutti

Chorus IN THE LORD PUT I MY TRUST
Chorus

Psalm xi 1

* Bar 11: Handel wrote d here. It seems likely that he omitted to change to f when he altered notes 2 and 3 in bar 10 from Bb c.

* Bar 30: Bsn and D.B. follow the Bass voice

11

* Bars 91-2: no text for Soprano in the autograph

* Bar 103: underlay follows the early copies. The autograph has 'bird' to note 1 of this bar.

* Bar 142: an unusual example of parallel octaves in Handel.

Solo GOD IS A CONSTANT SURE DEFENCE
Tenor Solo

Psalm ix 9

God is a con-stant sure de-fence a-gainst___ op-pres-sing rage, a-gainst op-pres-sing rage, a-gainst op-pres-sing rage,___ a-gainst___ op-pres-sing rage,

* Bar 38: see Preface for discussion of this cadence.

No.4   Chorus   BEHOLD THE WICKED BEND THEIR BOW
Chorus

Psalm xi 2

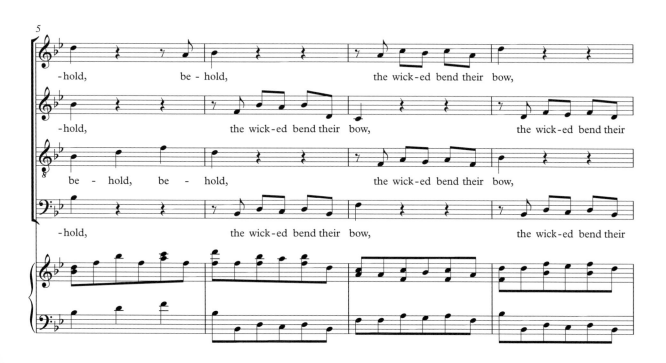

20

heart, the man of___ up - right heart.

heart, the man of___ up - right heart.

heart, the man of___ up - right heart.

heart, the man of___ up - right heart.

No.5   Solo   BUT GOD, WHO HEARS THE SUFF'RING POOR
Tenor solo

Psalm xii 5

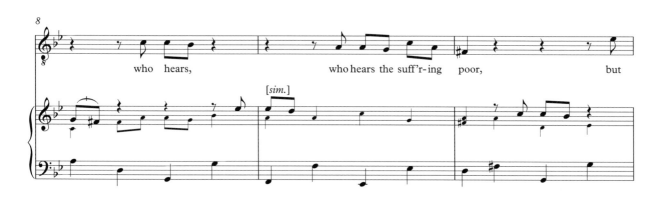

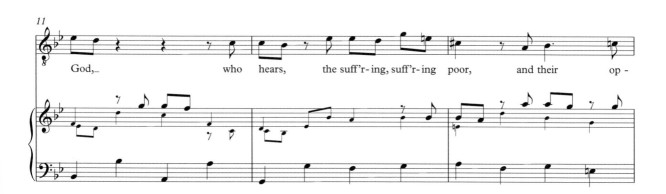

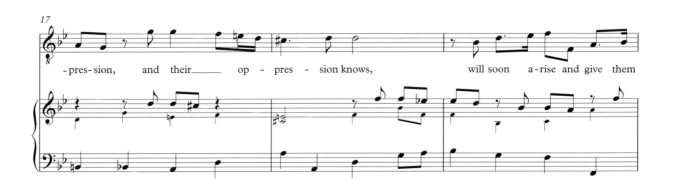

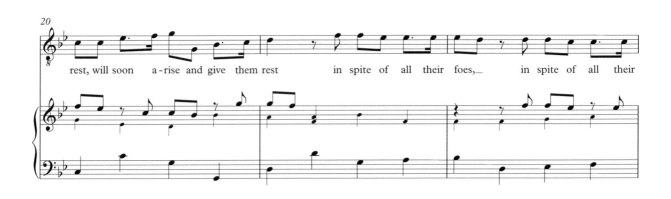

rest, will soon a-rise and give them rest, in spite,_ in

spite of all their foes, in spite_____ of_____ all their foes, of all their foes, in

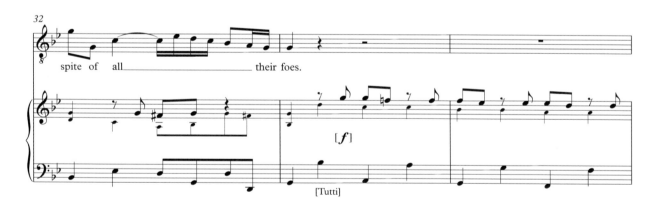

spite of all_____ their foes.

[f]

[Tutti]

[tr]

No.6   Chorus   SNARES, FIRE AND BRIMSTONES ON THEIR HEADS

Chorus

Psalm xi 6

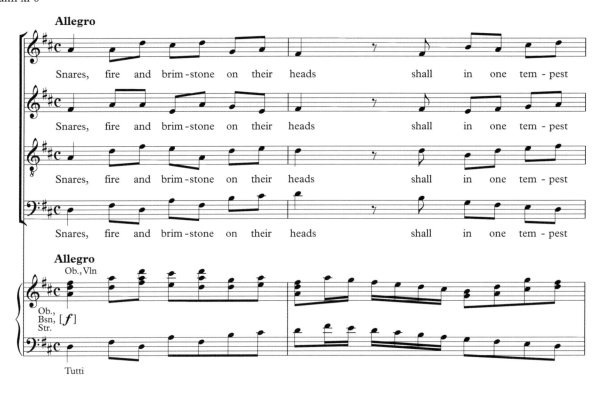

[senza D.B.]   [Tutti]

* Bar 33: the autograph and several other sources have c' sharp here. Handel changed the two preceeding notes from e' d'

No.7

Psalm xi 7

Solo THE RIGHTEOUS LORD
Tenor solo

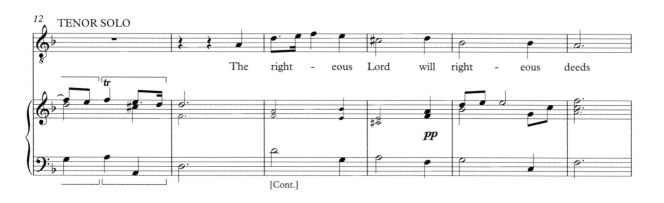

TENOR SOLO

The right - eous Lord will right - eous deeds

[Cont.]

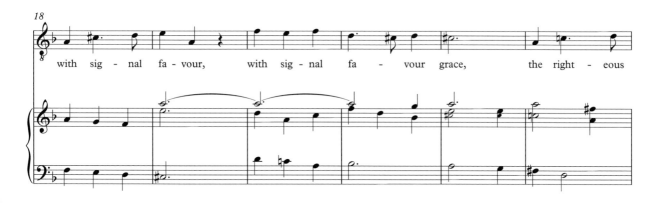

with sig - nal fa - vour, with sig - nal fa - vour grace, the right - eous

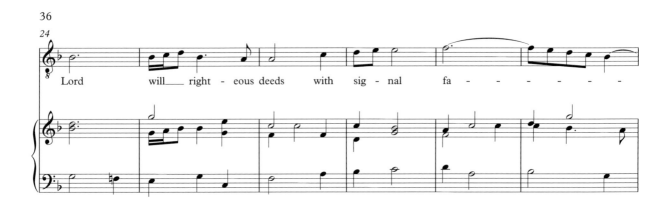

Lord will__ right - eous deeds with sig - nal fa - - - - - -

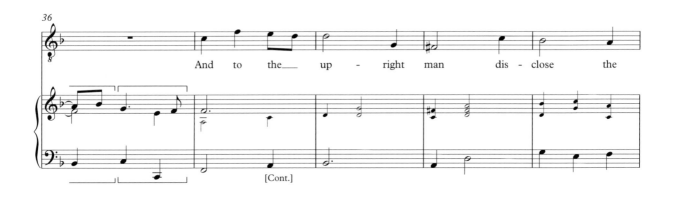

- - - - - vour grace.

[Tutti]

And to the__ up - right man dis - close the

[Cont.]

bright - ness of____ his face, and to the up - right

man___ dis - close   the   bright - ness of____ his___ face,   the

bright - ness of_____ his face,   and__

[Tutti]   [Cont.]

to   the   up - right man___ dis - close   the   bright - ness

of   his   face.

[mf]

[Tutti]

* Bar 58: This a' has no leger line in the autograph. It has been copied as f' in all later sources except **E**.

No.8   Chorus THEN SHALL MY SONG, WITH PRAISE INSPIR'D

Chorus

Psalm xiii 6

* Bar 27: Handel wrote d″ here; g″ follows the melodic pattern and avoids parallel fifths with the bass.

Cont.

* Bar 34: Oboe has e' here, clashing with Soprano f'.